CATS

Amanda O'Neill

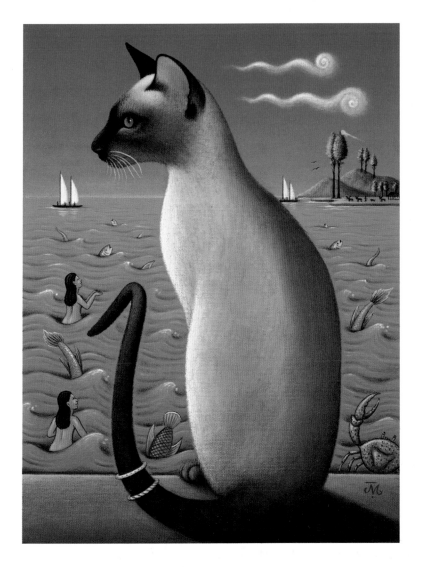

KING**f**ISHER

NEW YORK

To Conor and his cat, Jess

KINGFISHER
Larousse Kingfisher Chambers Inc.
95 Madison Avenue
New York, New York 10016

First published in 1998
10 9 8 7 6 5 4 3 2 1

LIBRARY OF CONGRESS CATALOGING-IN-PUBLICATION DATA
O'Neill, Amanda.
    Cats / Amanda O'Neill. — 1st ed.
        p.   cm.
    Includes index.
    Summary: Surveys the breeding, care, evolution, behavior,
mythology, and domestication of cats.
    1. Cats—Juvenile literature.   [1. Cats.]   I. Title.
SF445.7.06   1998
636.8—dc21   97-31739   CIP AC

ISBN 0-7534-5113-1

Editor: Clare Oliver
Design: Ben White Associates and Terry Woodley
Cover design: Terry Woodley
Cover illustration: Paul Stagg (Virgil Pomfret)
Art editors: Sue Aldworth and Ch'en Ling
Picture research: Veneta and Davina Bullen
Printed in Italy

CONTENTS

CAT FAMILY

From mighty lions to humble strays, cats form an instantly recognizable family. They may come in different sizes and colors, but all cats share the same graceful shape. Highly successful hunters, all species of cat are carnivores—they all eat meat.

▼ The shy marbled cat— a mini clouded leopard— is an endangered species. It is only slightly larger than most domestic (pet) cats.

◄ Despite its name, southern Asia's most common wild cat, the leopard cat, doesn't really look like its big cousin. It has rows of spots instead of the leopard's rosette patterns.

◄ A forest dweller that spends much of its life in the trees, the beautiful clouded leopard is smaller than a leopard. For its size, this cat has the biggest teeth of all the felines: it's nicknamed "the modern saber-tooth!"

▲ Little is known about the flat-headed cat, except that it hunts fish and frogs along forest riverbanks. Its long body, short legs, and flattened head make it look somewhat like a domestic cat that's been squashed!

The cat family can be divided into three groups. The smallest group (*Acinonyx*) contains only one species, the cheetah. The cheetah is classed on its own because it is the only cat to outrun its prey rather than stalk it. The two main cat groups are the big cats (*Panthera*), such as lions and tigers, and the little cats (*Felis*). Apart from size, the main distinction is that big cats roar and little cats purr. Some medium-sized cats, such as the clouded leopard, don't quite fit in with the big or little cats. Zoologists are still arguing about how to class these cats.

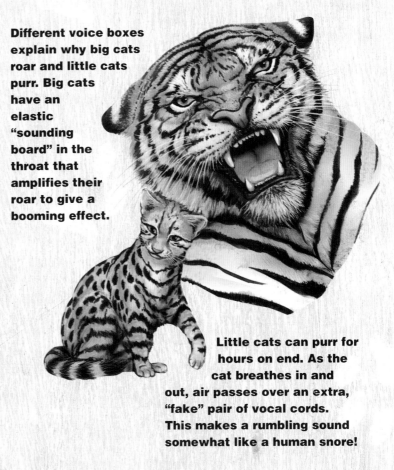

Different voice boxes explain why big cats roar and little cats purr. Big cats have an elastic "sounding board" in the throat that amplifies their roar to give a booming effect.

Little cats can purr for hours on end. As the cat breathes in and out, air passes over an extra, "fake" pair of vocal cords. This makes a rumbling sound somewhat like a human snore!

5

Evolution of the cat

The story of cats begins some sixty million years ago, with a small, weasel-like carnivore called *Miacis*. This was probably the ancestor of all modern carnivores, including dogs and bears as well as cats. The first recognizably catlike animal, *Dinictis*, evolved ten million years later. Its modern descendants include all the cats.

Distant cousins

Civets, genets, and mongooses (the *Viverridae* family) are also descended from *Dinictis*. So this genet is a distant cousin of the cat tribe—a closer relative than the bear or the dog.

genet

From little *Miacis* and medium-sized *Dinictis* sprang all cats, great and small. The modern cat family numbers 36 wild species.

Alongside the domestic cat (*Felis catus*), the other little cats include the African wildcat, black-footed cat, bobcat, cougar, fishing cat, jungle cat, lynx, manul, margay, ocelot, sand cat, and serval. The tiger, lion, leopard, and jaguar make up the big cats.

big cats, *Panthera*

little cats, *Felis*

Dinictis

true cats, *Felidae*

 *Miacis*

The cheetah isn't classed with the big cats or the little cats. It developed separately and became the world's fastest land animal. Its top recorded speed is 60 mph (96km/h).

cheetah, *Acinonyx*

saber-tooths

OLIGOCENE PERIOD		MIOCENE PERIOD	PLIOCENE PERIOD	
35 million years ago	25 million years ago		7 million years ago	2 million years ago

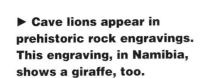

► Cave lions appear in prehistoric rock engravings. This engraving, in Namibia, shows a giraffe, too.

The early cat family split into two branches: saber-tooths and true cats. Saber-tooths were big and powerful, but relatively small-brained. They lived on Earth for almost thirty-four million years. The saber-tooths died out around twelve thousand years ago and left no modern descendants. The early true cats also included large animals such as the cave lion. Little cats evolved about twelve million years ago. As cats spread across the world, through Asia, Africa, Europe, and the Americas, a variety of species developed. The wildcat, ancestor of our pets, first appeared over one-and-a-half million years ago.

Fang monster

Saber-tooths, such as *Smilodon*, are so called because they had extremely long canine teeth. When they hunted mammoths and other large beasts, they used their canines like sabers (swords) to stab their prey.

Smilodon

The elastic skeleton

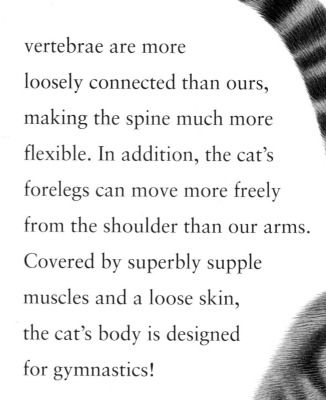

A cat's body is so flexible it seems almost boneless. It can twist and turn at incredible angles, stretch out for a streamlined pounce, or squeeze through the tiniest gap.

Bones are solid objects which can't really be elastic, so how does the cat manage this? The answer lies in the design of its skeleton. Like ours, the cat's backbone is made up of a chain of small bones called vertebrae. But the cat's vertebrae are more loosely connected than ours, making the spine much more flexible. In addition, the cat's forelegs can move more freely from the shoulder than our arms. Covered by superbly supple muscles and a loose skin, the cat's body is designed for gymnastics!

Cat workout

Artists have long been fascinated by the cat's suppleness. In this book, you'll see that there are as many ways of painting a cat as there are cats! These black-and-white drawings come from a book of picture stories about cats done by a French artist in the late 1800s. They celebrate the flowing curves into which cats twist their elastic bodies—whether they are awake or asleep.

◀ **"Paresse" from _Des Chats_, by Théophile Steinlen**

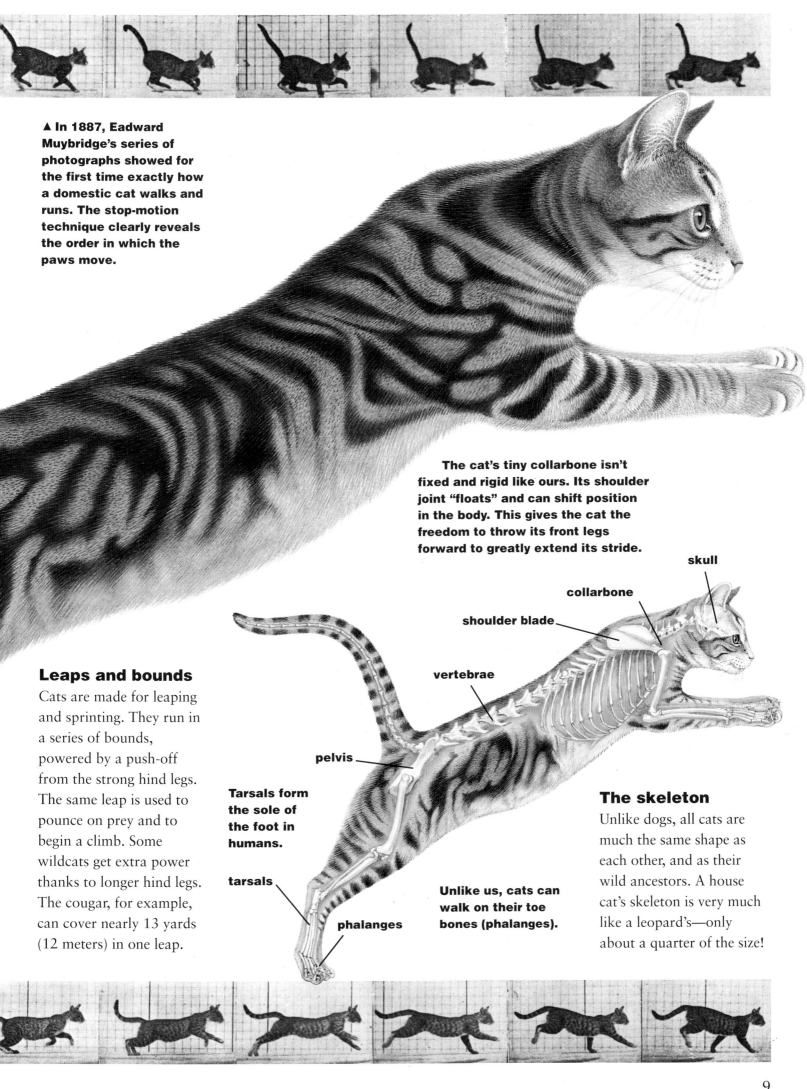

▲ In 1887, Eadward Muybridge's series of photographs showed for the first time exactly how a domestic cat walks and runs. The stop-motion technique clearly reveals the order in which the paws move.

The cat's tiny collarbone isn't fixed and rigid like ours. Its shoulder joint "floats" and can shift position in the body. This gives the cat the freedom to throw its front legs forward to greatly extend its stride.

skull

collarbone

shoulder blade

vertebrae

pelvis

Leaps and bounds

Cats are made for leaping and sprinting. They run in a series of bounds, powered by a push-off from the strong hind legs. The same leap is used to pounce on prey and to begin a climb. Some wildcats get extra power thanks to longer hind legs. The cougar, for example, can cover nearly 13 yards (12 meters) in one leap.

Tarsals form the sole of the foot in humans.

tarsals

phalanges

Unlike us, cats can walk on their toe bones (phalanges).

The skeleton

Unlike dogs, all cats are much the same shape as each other, and as their wild ancestors. A house cat's skeleton is very much like a leopard's—only about a quarter of the size!

Balancing tricks

Cats are never clumsy. A wonderful sense of balance allows them to climb to great heights or walk along the narrowest ledge. Even when cats do fall, they're famous for always landing on their feet—they have been known to survive a fall of 32 stories, without fatal injury.

The acrobat

Tightrope-walking the top of a narrow fence is easy for the cat, placing each paw exactly in front of the other. The cat can even turn around halfway without falling. To do this, it balances on its hind legs and pushes its forelegs as far back as possible, then shifts its weight to them before swinging its hindquarters around. Cats learn this skill as kittens, but practice makes perfect!

On your feet!

Flying cats and water form graceful curves in this unusual portrait of artist Salvador Dali. It took the photographer's four assistants and three good-natured cats 26 attempts to achieve this result!

▲ *Dali Atomicus,* by **Philippe Halsman**

1

Climbing

The cat begins its climb with a leap at the fence, then grabs hold with its claws. Having gotten a grip, it pulls itself up with its powerful forelegs. Coming down is harder: most cats prefer to jump than to ease down backward.

A safe landing

The cat uses its eyes and ears to make sure that it will always fall on its feet. In midair (1), the eyes and a finely-tuned balance organ in the ears send messages to the brain, identifying the direction of gravity's pull. Now the cat can pinpoint the exact position of its head in relation to the ground. The cat rights its head first (2), then twists its body into line until its feet point downward (3). The outstretched tail helps it to balance as it lands feetfirst (4).

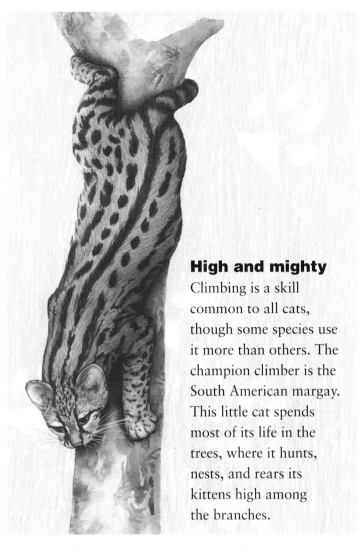

High and mighty

Climbing is a skill common to all cats, though some species use it more than others. The champion climber is the South American margay. This little cat spends most of its life in the trees, where it hunts, nests, and rears its kittens high among the branches.

Tree-climbing gives cats a high-rise hunting ground. So many birds and small animals feed in the branches that the treetop world is like a cats' supermarket! Trees also provide safe hiding places from a cat's enemies, lookout posts for spotting prey, and shelter from the sun's heat. Most little cat species are at home in the trees, but even lions are known to make use of this higher level.

11

Teeth and claws

Head of a hunter
A look at the cat's skull
shows us the teeth of a
meat-eater. They are
designed to bite, tear,
and chop, but not to
chew. Cats swallow
their food without
chewing it up. Instead,
the stomach breaks
down the food with
digestive juices.

The killing bite
Wild cats must kill in
order to live. A stabbing
blow from their long
canine teeth to the back of
the victim's neck brings a
quick death. Domestic
cats can kill in just the
same way as this leopard,
though in both cases
youngsters have to learn
how to deliver the killing
bite. Many pet cats never
master it.

A cat's teeth and claws
are its weapons for
fighting and its tools for hunting.
Long canine teeth—the cat family's
trademark—can hold and kill prey,
and tear meat. The back teeth serve
as cutlery, to cut food into manageable
pieces. The front teeth, the incisors, are
small, for nibbling. Sharp claws help to
give the cat a good grip on its prey.
They are also one of the reasons why
cats can climb so well: the cat uses
them as grappling hooks to hang
on as it works its way upward.

**Claws and teeth are deadly
weapons—so cats control their
use. Most cat fights involve more
screeching and glaring than
actual bites and scratches.**

Claws

Claws are too important to risk blunting them, so they are sheathed (1) when not in use. Small ligaments (bands of elastic tissue) attached to the toe bones hold the claws inside the paw. Larger ligaments pull back to let the claws flash out (2) when needed.

1

2

The cat's armory consists of 30 teeth (except for two wild species, the lynx and Pallas's cat, with 28 teeth each) and 18 claws—four on each hind paw and five on each forepaw with the fifth, the dew-claw, tucked up the back of each foreleg.

All cat species, except the cheetah, can sheathe (cover) their claws to protect the points. The fishing cat, however, doesn't quite have the full equipment. Its claws are too big for their sheaths, and don't tuck away completely.

Claw manicure

Claws grow throughout life, like our nails. When we see a cat scrape its claws down a tree (or a chair!), we often say it is sharpening its claws. It is actually stripping them—scratching off the worn outer coat of its claws to reveal new, sharp tips.

The fur coat

 More than just a coat, the cat's fur is a complete outfit! Like our clothes, it serves to keep out the cold—and excess heat. It is protective gear to save the skin from scratches and also camouflage gear, the color or pattern helping to hide the cat from its prey—or from enemies. Finally, the coat is a bulletin board which bears scent messages for other cats to "read." It also signals a threat when it is fluffed out in fear or anger, making the cat look bigger and fiercer.

Layers of hairs

Wildcats, and most domestic ones, wear a two-layered coat. The colorful and protective topcoat consists of long, strong guard hairs.

Next to the skin lies the undercoat of short, fluffy fur, like thermal underwear. This is made of down hairs, which are very short and soft, and awn hairs, slightly longer and coarser.

○ guard hair
● awn hair
○ down hair

Persian

Shorthair

Thick fur protects against the cold, especially when the cat fluffs up its coat. A layer of warm air gets trapped under the fur, next to the skin. This is like wearing thermal underwear. Of course, a pet cat can always come inside when it's had enough of the great outdoors!

Fur fashions

Pedigreed cats are bred for special kinds of coat. Shorthairs (1) have the same three-layered coat as their wild ancestors.

Persians (2) have extremely long fur, with no awn hairs. The Somali (3) is an example of a longhair with a medium-length fluffy coat (sometimes called a semi-longhair). Two unusual coat types belong to the American Wirehair (4), which has short, wavy, and wiry fur, and the Cornish Rex (5), whose coat is short, curly and without guard hairs. Strangest of all is the virtually hairless Sphynx (6), which doesn't even have whiskers.

Sandshoes

Going barefoot on scorching sand is very uncomfortable—and it's no different with bare paws. The sand cat lives in the deserts of Africa and Asia, and solves the problem by wearing furry slippers! Long tufts of fur protect its pads from the burning sand.

We don't wear winter coats in summer, and neither do cats. They adapt to the seasons by molting twice a year—they shed the old coat to grow a new one, which is thicker in winter and lighter in summer. Our domestic cats have lost some of this molting process. Most shed a few hairs all year round.

white	off-white	bluish white	pale bluish ivory	ivory	rich cream	buff cream	lavender	pale lavender	rich lavender

Cat colors

The first domestic cats were tabbies, like their wild ancestors. New colors developed gradually. Color breeding began in the 1800s. Before then, there were five basic colors (black, white, blue, cream, and red) plus tabby and tortoiseshell shades. Then color breeding really took off. Today we have more than 50 color varieties.

2 All-over color

Solid, or self-colored cats are a single color, with no shadings. Each hair is exactly the same color all down its length. Solid colors include black, blue, red, cream, lavender, and chocolate.

3 Soft shades

Shaded, shell, and smoke patterns are two-tone coats. In longhairs the color seems to change as the cat moves.

Colored tips

Shaded, shell, and smoke colors differ in the length of dark tip on each hair. Shaded coats (1) have more of a tip than shell, and smoke (2) have most of all. Ticked, or agouti coats are banded along the length of every hair (3).

KEY TO COATS
1 Mackerel Tabby
2 Russian Blue
3 Cream Shaded Cameo
4 Tortoiseshell
5 Ruddy Abyssinian
6 Chocolate-Point Siamese

1 Tabby types

Tabbies combine dark hairs with hairs banded in a dark and a pale color. The solid dark hairs may be grouped in stripes (mackerel), or patches (blotched), or rows of spots (spotted).

medium blue	bright blue	deep blue-gray	very deep blue	deep steel blue	pale cream-fawn	warm beige	warm fawn	light bronze	rich tawny brown

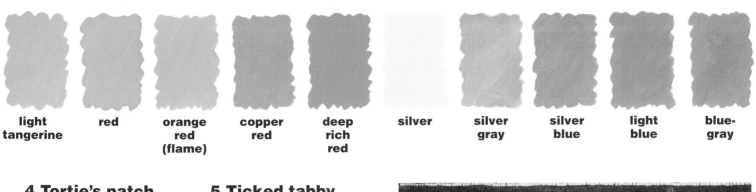

light tangerine	red	orange red (flame)	copper red	deep rich red	silver	silver gray	silver blue	light blue	blue-gray

4 Tortie's patch

Tortoiseshells are also two-tone, but in a patchwork pattern, often black, red, and cream.

5 Ticked tabby

The Abyssinian is a tabby in disguise! Its hairs are color-banded (ticked, or agouti), but there are no black hairs to form a tabby pattern, except on the face (and sometimes on the legs and tail).

▲ **A Roman mosaic shows the oldest tabby pattern, the mackerel. The blotched tabby did not** appear until around 1200. It was first seen in England and soon spread around the world.

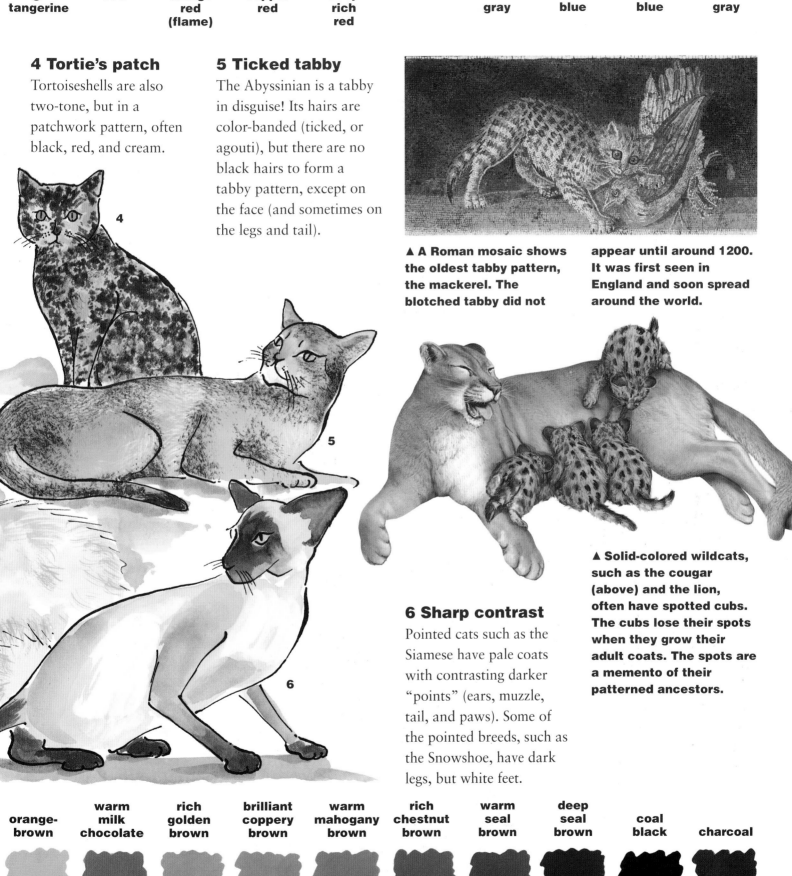

6 Sharp contrast

Pointed cats such as the Siamese have pale coats with contrasting darker "points" (ears, muzzle, tail, and paws). Some of the pointed breeds, such as the Snowshoe, have dark legs, but white feet.

▲ **Solid-colored wildcats, such as the cougar (above) and the lion, often have spotted cubs. The cubs lose their spots when they grow their adult coats. The spots are a memento of their patterned ancestors.**

orange-brown	warm milk chocolate	rich golden brown	brilliant coppery brown	warm mahogany brown	rich chestnut brown	warm seal brown	deep seal brown	coal black	charcoal

Cats' eyes

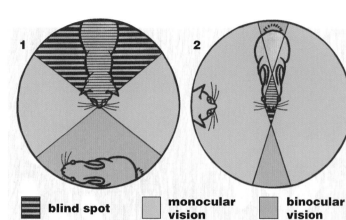 **S**ight is very important to cats. Their eyes are hunters' eyes—large, and designed for spotting prey. They are particularly alert to sudden movements.

Lynx-eyed

The sharp-eyed lynx can spot a grouse from 330 yards (300 meters) away —longer than three football fields. In ancient times this cat was a symbol of acute sight, and we still describe observant people as "lynx-eyed." Actually, most members of the cat family have equally good vision.

1 **2**

	blind spot		**monocular vision**		**binocular vision**

For sharp focus, an object needs to be seen by both eyes at once. This is binocular ("two-eyed") vision. Focusing with only one eye (monocular vision) picks out movement, but not distance.

Cats (1) have a very wide binocular area of vision, for sharp focus on their prey. In contrast, rabbits (2) have a much wider field of monocular vision—making it harder for hunters to creep up on them unseen.

Cats' vision differs from ours in several ways. They can see in light at least six times dimmer than we can, though even cats can't see in pitch darkness. They can't make out fine detail and small objects as well as we do, but they don't need to. Their color vision isn't as good, either; but they aren't color-blind, as was once thought.

1 **2** **3**

Eye-opener

At night, the pupils of a cat's eye open wide to let in maximum light (top). By day, they can avoid dazzle by narrowing to slits (bottom). Human eyes also adapt to light and dark, but not enough to cope with the near-darkness in which cats can see.

Night vision is aided by a "mirror" (tapetum) at the back of the eye, that reflects what light there is.

An eye-shield

Extra protection for the cat's eyes comes from the third eyelid, known as the haw, or nictitating membrane. This is tucked away in the inner corner of each eye, moving across the eye occasionally to spread moisture over the surface. Most of the time it stays out of sight.

A cat whose third eyelids are permanently on display is showing signs of illness and needs to visit the vet.

Eye colors

Domestic cats' eyes show an amazing color range. Pedigreed cats must have the approved eye color for their breed—blue for Siamese (1), and green for Chinchillas (3). Orange and yellow shades range from the Blue Persian's deep copper (2) to the Black Shorthair's gold (4). The Tabby Maine Coon (6) has hazel eyes, and the Odd-Eyed White Persian (5) has one blue eye and one orange!

Cats' eyes don't change just to cope with different lighting conditions, but also to react to different situations. A cat threatening an enemy narrows its pupils more tightly to focus on the foe, but a threatened cat opens its eyes wide in a black-eyed stare. In both cases, the eyes are displaying a warning signal as clear as any words!

4

5

6

Whiskers are high-powered organs of touch. They can even detect air movements.

Large, mobile ears can turn toward a sound to pinpoint its source. The cat's ears can even pick up high-pitched sounds (such as a mouse's squeak) that humans cannot hear.

The cat's sense of smell is 30 times better than that of a human.

Taste matters less to cats than to us. As carnivores, cats have taste buds that identify meaty and fatty tastes. We humans have 18 times more taste buds, so we can identify more types of taste than cats can.

Extra senses

Our simple world of five senses would seem boring to a cat. Whatever the claims for their "sixth sense" special powers, they definitely have one extra sense! A special organ in the roof of the mouth, the Jacobsen's organ, can "taste" scent particles in the air.

More senses

A hunter needs good hearing as well as good eyesight, and a cat's ears are designed for the job. The cat has an excellent sense of smell, too, though it doesn't rely on this to hunt. It uses its nose mainly to investigate food, and to "read" the smell messages produced by other cats. The cat doesn't need much sense of taste, but its sense of touch is highly developed, with sensitive whiskers (on its wrists as well as its face) acting as feelers.

No place like home
Cats also have a special homing mechanism. Far from home, the cat's built-in "compass" allows it to find its way back. Scientists are still investigating how this works. Sooty the cat hit the news when she trekked 100 miles (160km) to return to her old home after her owners moved to a new house. Sooty was sedated for the original car journey from Swansea, Wales, to Bath, England, but somehow still found her way back to Wales. Her amazing journey took six months!

Whisker work

As the cat pounces, its whiskers point forward to "read" the shape, size, and movements of its target.

Big ears

Its oversized ears tell us that the serval, an African wildcat, depends on its hearing to find its prey. The faintest rustle in the grass allows it to pinpoint the location of a hidden mouse or rat—and pounce! Those sensitive ears can even pick up the sound of a mole rat tunneling underground, so the serval knows just where to dig for dinner.

Cats' whiskers are highly sensitive feelers. With whiskers leading the way, the cat can detect the exact position, shape, and size of everything it approaches—even in the dark. This helps it to pounce accurately on prey and to know instantly whether a gap is wide enough to slip through. It also explains why cats don't bump into things the way we clumsy humans do.

CAT LIFE

Are cats loners? Their independence is legendary—there is even a Rudyard Kipling story called "The Cat that Walked by Himself." But cats really do enjoy company. In the wild, they may not form packs like dogs, but they usually live in family groups. And pet cats, kept individually or in pairs, are very content with their human family. Wild or tame, cats detest outsiders. Trespassers on their home territory will soon be chased away. That's why it can be difficult to introduce a second cat into your home.

When cats wash other family members, they leave scent traces on each other's coats. As a result, a shared "family smell" identifies them as a group.

Stay off my turf!

A cat considers the area around its home to be its territory, and will fight off trespassers. Males claim a large area, while females and neuters may stick to their own backyards. The two neuters above keep the peace by creating a no-man's-land between their territories.

22

Like people, cats have laws to help them live together peacefully. The rules of cat society are based on "knowing one's place." It's similar to the army: everyone knows their rank and gives way to those higher up. Breeding animals rank higher than neuters; tough cats outrank timid ones. But rank depends very much on territory: a cat may be boss on its home turf, but not next door.

Tumbling kittens enjoying a play-fight are also working out what their rank will be in adult life. "Top Cat" has to start out by becoming "Top Kitten" in the litter! At this age, they can settle who's boss without hurting each other—and, of course, have fun at the same time.

The way a cat moves, stands, and even sits says a lot. A confident cat walks tall, with its tail erect, or relaxes in comfort. A timid cat cowers to make itself as small as possible.

Cat chat

You might think that cats can't talk, but cats use no fewer than four languages to speak to one another: body language, voice, the faces they make, and smell. The scent of a cat's fur reveals to other cats its family and even what kind of mood it is in. All this information is beyond the reach of our much poorer sense of smell—apart from the powerful odor that tells us a tomcat has left his mark!

neutral **defensive** **aggressive** **content** **curious**

A look says it all

Ears, eyes, and mouth all work to make up the language of the face. On the defensive, ears flatten, pupils widen, and lips tighten. The aggressive cat puts up warning signals: drawn-back ears and slitted pupils. When contented, the cat switches off, with eyes almost closed. By contrast, a curious cat turns its senses on full: eyes, ears, and whiskers are all alert.

Cats use urine and scent from their glands to leave smell markers all around their territory, and they refresh these "signatures" every day or two. Other cats can "read" these markers to find out *who* has been visiting, *when*, and maybe even *why*— and they will often add a smelly note of their own.

▲ *A Musical Gathering of Cats*, by Ferdinand Van Kessell

The cat's scent glands are on the muzzle and temples, as well as at the base of the tail. By rubbing them against a tree trunk (or a human's legs) the cat leaves behind a message: "Mine! Keep your paws off."

Listen to me!

"Caterwauling"—that's how we describe tuneless singing or noisy quarreling. We find feline yowls very unmusical—and so do cats! From fighting howls to a cornered cat's low, husky threat-wails, these sounds are *meant* to put other cats off. But the cat's "conversational" sounds are much more pleasant. The cat "word" we know best is the meow, which is a demand for attention. This is both the kitten's call to Mom, and the adult cat's demand to its owner—"Let me in!" or "Feed me!" The greeting chirrup is also used between cats and by cats to humans. And of course there is the purr, used like the human smile—not only to show happiness but to indicate the absence of any threat.

25

Hunting machine

The whole cat family evolved as specialist hunters. It's not just lions and tigers who go for the kill. Hunting is so much a part of being a cat that even well-fed pets with no need to work for their supper often feel the urge to stalk mice and birds. Keen hunters, especially females, may even bring prey home to you—and expect you to be thrilled! Kittens learn hunting skills from their mothers, so if dead mice upset you, look for a kitten whose mom isn't interested in hunting.

Hunter's homework
A kitten's first kill may not be all its own work! Mother cats often bring live mice home for their kittens' play—and their education. Baby hunters have to learn to pounce accurately on their prey, hold it with their claws, and deliver the killing bite. Tossing a mouse in the air and swatting it down again is also good training for catching birds. It takes plenty of practice before a kitten's hunting technique becomes perfect.

A curious cat and a bold bird! Not all cats are keen hunters—but they all like to investigate small, moving objects.

► The paws are raised to trap the bird in mid-air and pull it down. At least, that's the theory—somehow he's missed!

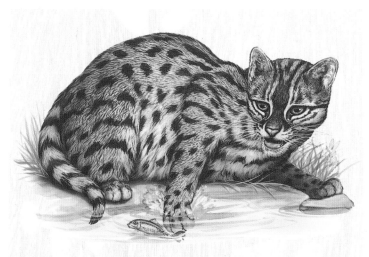

► Thousands of years of life among humans haven't spoiled the cat's hunting skills. During a 24-year career in a Scottish whisky distillery, Towser (1963–1987) caught an amazing 28,899 mice —that's just over a hundred a month!

Gone fishing!

Some pet cats learn to scoop fish out of the water. But the wild fishing cat of southern Asia is the real expert! Although it also hunts on land, taking prey as large as sheep, its speciality is the water.

Sometimes it does "fish" from the riverbank like our pets, but it also swims out to catch a fish, a frog, or even a duck for dinner. To help push itself through the water, the fishing cat even has partly webbed feet!

◄ Hunting made ship's cat Simon a hero of World War II! When the British ship HMS *Amethyst* was hit by enemy fire, Simon ignored his wounds and continued hunting for rats, protecting precious food supplies for three months while the battered ship was trapped. Simon received the Dickin Medal (a special British award for brave animals) in recognition of his war work; he is the only cat to ever receive this honor.

▼ Missed again? Well, he's not really trying! He's just using those sensitive paws to get the bird to join his game.

► Time to practice some patient stalking. Of course, he would prefer a chair leg or some long grass for cover.

► Let's try a pounce! At least that made the bird take notice—only it's taken flight, too. Oh well, who wants to catch birds anyway?

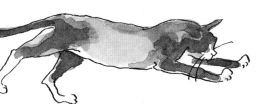

Playtime!

 One of the great pleasures of having a cat is its playful nature. For kittens, play is their schoolwork. Roughhousing with littermates teaches cat manners. Stalking Mom's tail or "killing" a toy teaches hunting skills. Wild chases around the furniture are like gym class! Cats never outgrow this playfulness. Adult cats play to stay fit— and also just for the fun of it.

Toys

Playthings range from a scrap of crumpled-up paper to designer toys from pet stores. Moving objects, thrown or dangled on a string, are always appealing. Make sure toys are safe. A ball of yarn may be irresistible, but it can be dangerous to a kitten who swallows a length or catches a claw. Check stuffed toys such as catnip mice to make sure that their eyes, ears, and tails are secure and can't be swallowed.

Faithful retriever

 We don't usually expect cats to play a game of "Fetch" like dogs. But some, such as the wild-looking Abyssinian, thoroughly enjoy retrieving a ball. If your cat is one of these breeds, you'll probably be worn out before it is!

Make time in your day to play with your cat. Joining in its games helps to strengthen the bond between you.

Quieter cats often prefer hunting games, stalking a toy (or the tie on your bathrobe) and pouncing on it. You can add to the excitement by making the toy move like real prey!

Kittens' play is enchanting to watch— and to join in with. But it's also serious business. Chasing a small, moving toy is good practice for mousework later.

The destroyer

Oriental cats such as Burmese need a lot of entertaining. Like small children, they can cause complete chaos if they're left to amuse themselves. And scolding won't help them understand that torn curtains are their fault. It will just upset them—they were only playing! If you own a highly active cat, provide lots of exercise to use up its energy.

Water sports

Swimming isn't a common cat pastime, but the Turkish Van (known as the "swimming cat") is renowned for it. This cat takes its name from Lake Van in southeast Turkey, where it comes from. Even the Van kitten enjoys splashing around.

Very active cats (especially Oriental breeds like Siamese and Burmese) enjoy games that involve climbing, jumping, and racing around. These are solo games, but sofas and curtains can suffer during these crazy dashes, so you may want to distract them with a toy! Team games for cats tend to focus on playfighting, and kittens have to learn to control their teeth and claws when tackling thinner human skin.

Body beautiful

In the wild, cats that don't stay fit starve. Even though domestic cats have trained humans to look after them now, they still take great care of their health. They exercise regularly and indulge in plenty of long snoozes. They enjoy a balanced diet, and they try to keep themselves spotlessly clean—sometimes with some help from their friends.

The cat's comb

The cat's tongue is a very special tool. If *you* licked a cat's fur, you would just make it wet! But when a cat licks its fur it is actually combing it. Its tongue is covered with tiny spines, which work just like the teeth on our combs to tease out tangles and remove dead hairs.

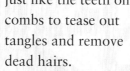

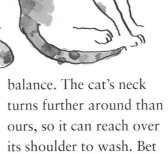

How to wash

Even a cat can't lick the top of its head! Instead, it wets its forepaw with its tongue to use like a washcloth. The cat can reach almost every part of its body. Underneath calls for a "yoga" position, with one leg in the air for balance. The cat's neck turns further around than ours, so it can reach over its shoulder to wash. Bet you can't lick your back! The small front teeth (the incisors) come in handy to nibble out grass seeds or tangles from the tail. Bathtime over!

Like us, cats need their beauty sleep—and here they are real experts. Cats spend two-thirds of their lives dozing! But instead of having a set bedtime, they curl up whenever they please, day or night.

If a sleeping cat is all curled up, it is just enjoying a catnap! In this light sleep its senses are still alert, and it can spring to life in an instant. When it's in light sleep, the animal may drift into several minutes of deep sleep. During deep sleep, it uncurls its body and goes completely floppy. You may also see it twitching, which means the cat is dreaming!

Cats can twist around to wash nearly every part of their body, but sometimes a friend will help. When cats wash each other, they are telling each other that they are good friends. They are also spreading their scent on each other, producing a shared "family smell" —like a badge that says they belong to the same club! A human stroking a cat delivers the same message of friendship and belonging.

▲ *The Cat*, by Tsugouharu Foujita

Bringing up baby

Whether she has just one kitten, the usual four kittens, or more than a dozen, the cat is a devoted mother. She chooses a safe, quiet nursery for her helpless babies, and rarely leaves them for the first couple of days. Once they start toddling around, she has her work cut out to keep them out of trouble.

1 Newborn

A gentle rubdown from Mom's tongue gets the newborn kitten to start breathing. Its eyes and ears are sealed, but its nose is working—ready to locate the milk supply.

2 Mother's milk

Like all baby mammals, kittens need their mother's milk—and not just for its food value. The first milk she produces for them contains vital protection against disease.

Mother love

Kittens need a lot of care, protection, and teaching. For eight weeks their mother is their food supply, nurse, guardian, jungle gym, and favorite playmate. It's hard work! In real life, she is likely to be more patient than the mother in this Victorian painting looks!

▲ *Playing With Mother,* by Horatio Cauldery

3 Carried away

A few days after the birth, the mother often carries her kittens to a new nest. It's a habit leftover from the wild, where staying in one place for too long could attract the attention of predators.

Foster mom

Mother love is so strong that cats may even adopt outsiders into a litter. Cats' foster babies range from rats and puppies to zoo orphans such as marmosets!

▼ **Beauty the cat feeds Sammy the squirrel along with her own three kittens.**

Kittens are ready to leave home when they are eight to twelve weeks old. At this stage they are still babies, and need special care from the new owner. This includes four small meals a day, lessons in cat manners, and lots of attention. In the wild, they would stay with their mother until they could hunt like adults. Big cat species take the longest to grow up. A tiger may stay with Mom for as long as four years!

6 Grown-up dinner

Kittens discover solid food at four to five weeks old, moving on to it gradually. At six to eight weeks, mother's milk comes off the menu completely.

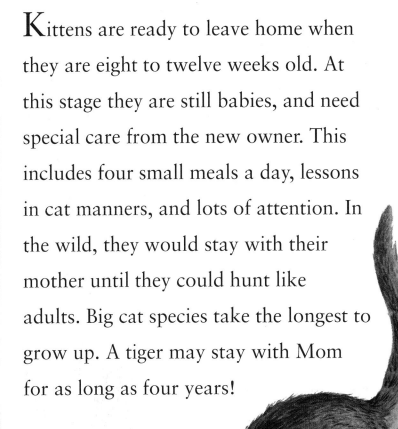

4 I spy...

Kittens' eyes start to open at between four and ten days old. It takes about three days for the eyes to open fully. Even so, their vision stays fuzzy for a couple of weeks.

5 Roughhousing

Kittens start to toddle when they are about three weeks old. A week later, they are steady on their feet and ready to learn the skill of washing themselves. They also discover how to play!

YOU AND YOUR CAT

Wildcats look after themselves, but your pet depends on you for many of its needs, such as food, grooming, healthcare—and affection! A visit to the vet may not be your cat's idea of fun, but it is an essential part of cat care.

Your cat needs to be vaccinated against common killer diseases such as cat flu and feline enteritis.

Another essential veterinary treatment for pet cats is neutering, to prevent breeding. There are too many kittens needing homes already. Neutering also makes the cat less likely to stray—and gets rid of the strong smell of a tom!

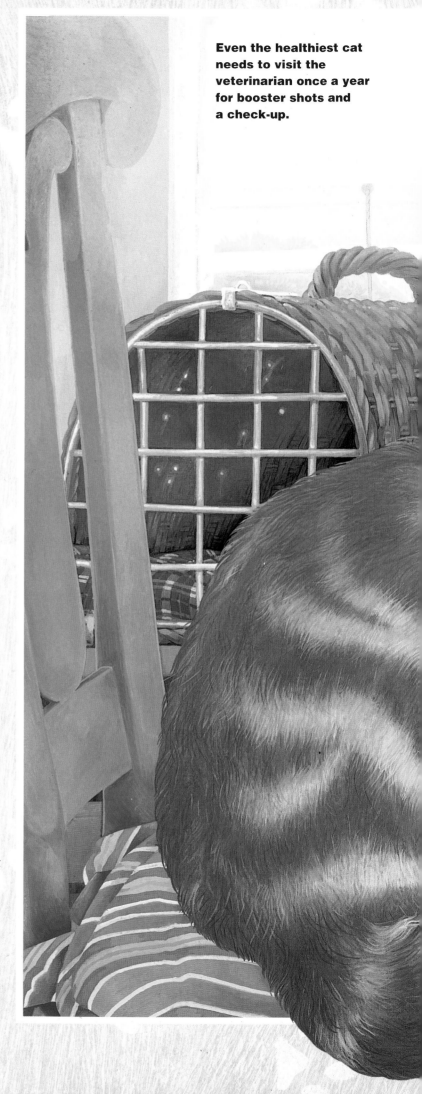

Even the healthiest cat needs to visit the veterinarian once a year for booster shots and a check-up.

Unwanted guests

cat flea

Even the best-kept cats pick up fleas and parasitic worms from time to time. Fleas are easily seen in the fur, and so are their tiny red-black droppings. Flea powder, sprays, or drops are the answer—but it's **roundworm** necessary to de-flea the whole house, not just your pet. Worms, such as tapeworms and roundworms, live inside the cat, so they're less obvious. Play it safe and ask your vet for regular doses of worm pills. Worms can infect us, too, so wash your hands after handling your pet.

34

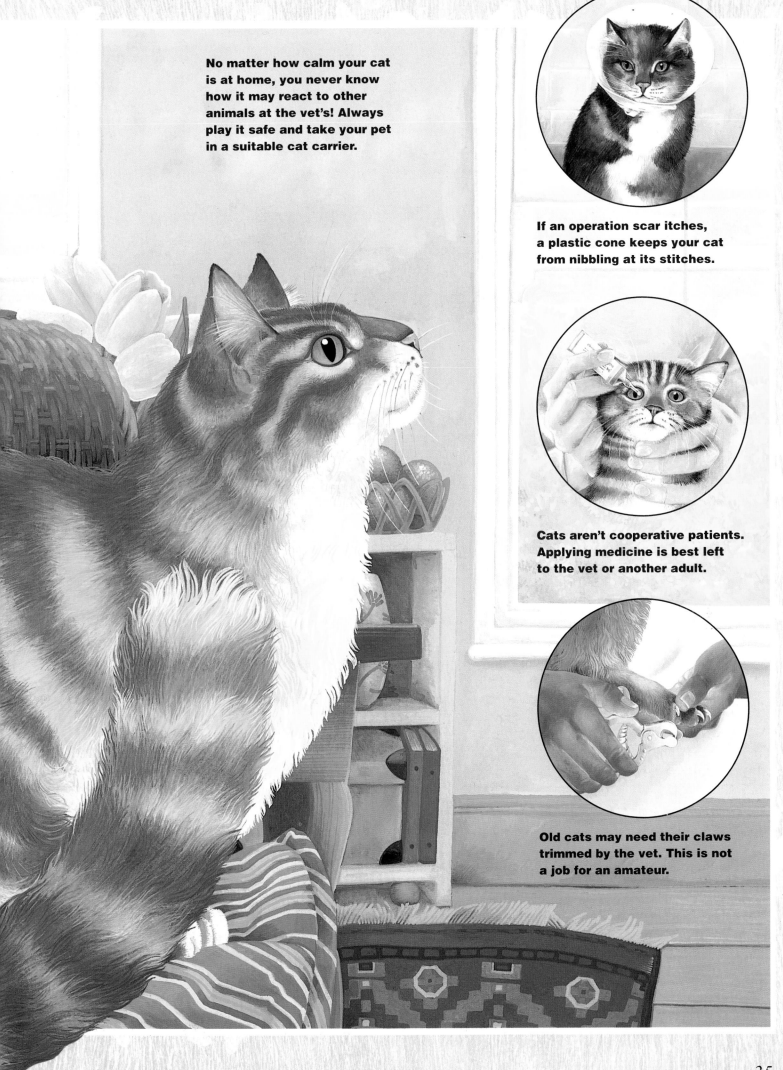

No matter how calm your cat is at home, you never know how it may react to other animals at the vet's! Always play it safe and take your pet in a suitable cat carrier.

If an operation scar itches, a plastic cone keeps your cat from nibbling at its stitches.

Cats aren't cooperative patients. Applying medicine is best left to the vet or another adult.

Old cats may need their claws trimmed by the vet. This is not a job for an amateur.

clean
ears

bright
eyes

clean
nose
(a runny
nose could
indicate flu)

clean teeth
and gums

clean, well
cared-for
fur, with
no flea
droppings

rounded
body, not
too thin
or too fat
(a pot
belly
suggests
worms)

good
temperament
(nervous or
aggressive
kittens make
poor pets)

plenty of bounce: a
healthy kitten is alert
and ready for fun

Choosing a cat

Your cat may be a member of your family for as long as 20 years, so it makes sense to choose carefully! Look for a healthy, active animal with a friendly attitude to ensure a good start. Males or females make equally good pets when neutered. Either a kitten or an adult cat might be perfect for you. Kittens are irresistible but have a lot to learn, like housebreaking and claw control. Adults are usually better behaved, but need time to settle into a new home.

A good start

A caring breeder will produce healthy kittens. Make sure that the mother cat has been well-treated and that the kittens are used to people. The breeder should have de-wormed the kittens, and should not allow them to leave home too young—they should be at least eight weeks old.

One or two?

If your kitten will be left alone all day, it may be kinder to have two, to keep each other company. But one cat will be perfectly happy as long as its needs are met. Two kittens may be twice as much fun—but also twice the cost in neutering, vaccinations, and food.

Singapura

Siamese

Persian

Ragdoll

Pedigreed breeds

If you are considering getting a pedigreed cat, take the time to learn about the breed first. It's true that cat breeds vary less than dog breeds. There are no real giants or miniatures, though a Ragdoll (one of the biggest breeds) may weigh five times as much as a tiny Singapura. Most breeds have the same basic shape, but vary from slender to stout. Compare the Siamese (long legs, body, and head) with the Persian (short legs, body, and face).

There are two main considerations when choosing a pedigreed cat. First, do you have time to groom your cat every day? Daily detangling is essential for a longhair. Shorthairs, on the other hand, have easy-care coats.

The one thing that varies hugely between pedigreed breeds is temperament. Persians and Ragdolls tend to be laid-back and very relaxed. The Singapura is rather shy, while the Siamese is notoriously loud and attention-seeking.

Pet store kittens

Kittens in a pet store window are tempting, but it's safer and kinder to get your kitten direct from its breeder. Caring breeders don't sell to pet stores. A stay in a pet store between homes is unsettling for a baby animal and exposes it to a wide range of germs.

Cat rescue

It can be very rewarding to adopt a homeless cat from a rescue shelter. These charities normally check out the health and character of cats before re-housing them, and go to some trouble to match animals with suitable owners. They may charge an adoption fee.

The common non-pedigreed cat is the basic model of cat. Using this as a starting point, pedigreed cats have been bred to emphasize particular ingredients of appearance and character. Special features such as really long fur, pointed markings, or bright blue eyes are unlikely to appear in non-pedigreed cats. But both pedigreed and non-pedigreed cats offer a rainbow variety of colors and characters. Whichever cat or kitten you choose will make an equally lovable companion.

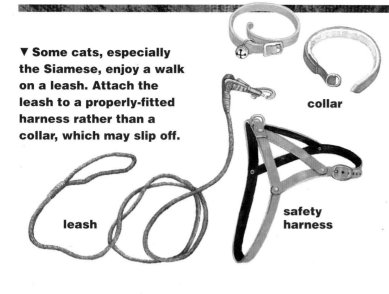

▼ Some cats, especially the Siamese, enjoy a walk on a leash. Attach the leash to a properly-fitted harness rather than a collar, which may slip off.

collar

leash

safety harness

Cat equipment

P et stores sell a bewildering variety of accessories for cats. Don't worry, you won't need all of them! Some things you can do without, and some you can make yourself: an old, soft towel makes a comfy bed, and paper towel rolls are always popular toys. If your cat is going to live indoors, it will have some special needs. For example, a scratching post for its claws and a pot of grass to help keep it healthy.

scratching post

▼ Outdoor cats nibble grass, which helps them digest their dinners. Indoor cats shouldn't miss out: grow a pot of grass on a windowsill for them.

grass

flea spray

comb

toys

brush and comb

I'm home!

A flap fitted in a door will allow your cat to come and go as it chooses. It also saves all that meowing on the doorstep!

kitty door

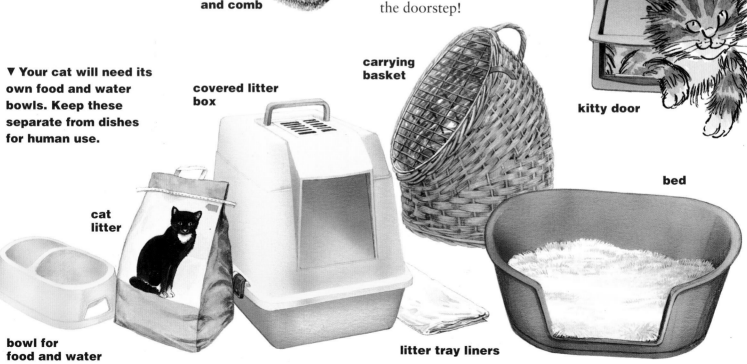

▼ Your cat will need its own food and water bowls. Keep these separate from dishes for human use.

covered litter box

carrying basket

cat litter

bed

bowl for food and water

litter tray liners

▲ A collar with an identification tag may save your pet if it strays. Be sure to choose a safety collar, which has an elastic strip, so that if it catches on a branch your cat can wriggle free.

Cat carriage

Suitable carriers come in plastic, fiberglass, wicker, or even strong cardboard. You will need a carrier to ensure your cat's safety during trips to the vet (or anywhere else). It's not a good idea for your pet to only associate the carrier with going to the vet! Get the carrier out at other times, too; and let your cat get used to it.

Cat bathroom

A litter box is a must for kittens and adult cats that are kept indoors. Keep it in a quiet corner, not too near your pet's food bowl. They can be open or covered—a cover gives your pet more privacy and helps contain the smell! Even so, it will need cleaning every day. It's a good idea to check what type of litter a new kitten has been used to, as a sudden change may confuse it.

LITTER
1 fuller's earth
2 chalk
3 wood chips

litter scoop

▼ Claws need a regular workout, and providing a scratching post may save the furniture! A platform on top means the post doubles as a jungle gym and a play center.

Sleep easy

Pet stores stock a wide range of cat beds, from open plastic baskets to furry igloos. Some cats prefer to find their own bed—or share yours! Wherever your cat sleeps, its bedding will need regular washing and flea checks.

Cat care

Your cat's health depends on regular, well-balanced meals. Adult cats should be fed twice a day and will almost certainly remind you when it's mealtime! Growing kittens need several smaller meals a day, to suit their smaller stomachs.

If your cat is a longhair, remember to groom it daily. Shorthairs need brushing only once or twice a week to remove dead hairs. Grooming time is also when you will spot any injuries, early signs of illness, or fleas. Best of all, it helps you to bond with your cat, who will enjoy the attention.

▲ *The Cat,*
by Fernando Botero

Fat cat
A fat cat is not a healthy cat. If your cat is over-weight, ask your vet for advice on a reducing diet. It could be that you are overfeeding your cat, or your cat may be tricking your neighbors into supplying extra meals! Like humans, some cats put on weight because they have a lazy lifestyle. Indoor cats especially need plenty of play.

A healthy diet
Cats need cat food! Dog food or household scraps don't contain the high level of animal protein they need—and even milk upsets many cats' stomachs. Choose either canned cat food, a scientifically-balanced dry food, or cooked fish. Make sure there's always fresh water, too.

For a cat whose tail gets in the cream, breakfast and bathtime come together! Most cats love a lick of cream but it should be given only as an occasional treat.

Grooming matters

Grooming is more than beauty care. Longhairs depend on daily brushing to prevent tangles that, if neglected, may need to be clipped out by the vet.

Brush the fur gently, without tugging. Go against the way it naturally lies, lifting the fur upward and outward so that you work right to the roots. A comb is useful for lifting out dead hair.

Finish off the cat's face fur and neck ruff with a smaller brush. An old toothbrush is ideal for this delicate work—but please don't borrow one from the bathroom!

Great balls of fur

Loose hairs get swallowed when a cat licks its coat, and can build up in the stomach. There's no need to worry unless your pet can't get rid of its fur balls. If you spot the danger signs of a dry cough and loss of appetite, head for the vet. But remember, prevention is better than cure: regular brushing means fewer dead hairs for your cat to swallow.

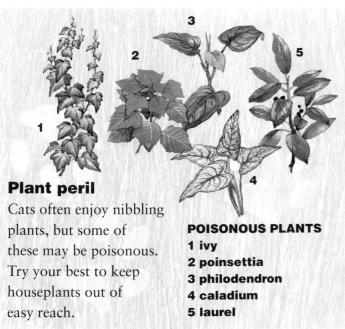

Plant peril

Cats often enjoy nibbling plants, but some of these may be poisonous. Try your best to keep houseplants out of easy reach.

POISONOUS PLANTS
1 ivy
2 poinsettia
3 philodendron
4 caladium
5 laurel

To make sure that curiosity doesn't kill your cat, check the house for dangers. Tuck electrical cords out of the way where they can't be chewed, and remember to put away poisonous household chemicals such as bleach. With a new cat or kitten, it's a good idea to protect your home also, by moving breakable ornaments and houseplants.

Understanding your cat

Cats can't speak our language, and we can't speak Cat. But that won't stop your pet from telling you its needs, wishes, and opinions in its own way. And, with a little patience, you can learn to treat the cats you meet politely—on their terms.

▲ George Adamson with Boy, one of the lions he rescued from zoo imprisonment in 1965.

Lion's share

When we make the effort to understand a cat, it will respond with affection—even if it happens to be a member of the big cat group. The film *Born Free* tells the story of the friendship between Joy and George Adamson and the lions who shared their lives. Here George and his "best-friend" lion, Boy, enjoy a walk through the African bush.

One way to a cat's heart is through its stomach! By providing food, you are telling your cat that you are its friend. But there's more to friendship than food. Cats need affection, too—and will give plenty in return.

Making friends

When visitors come, cats always seem to make a beeline for the one person who doesn't like cats. This should tell you how to approach a strange cat: don't! Cats don't like pushy people, so sit back, wait patiently, and let Kitty make the first move.

Don't stare! It's not polite —and in cat language, it's a threat. Look slightly away, or try a couple of slow blinks to say, "I mean you no harm."

To a cat, you're huge—so make yourself smaller, and less scary, by crouching down. Hold out one hand to invite Kitty to come and investigate.

After a sniff, the cat will rub its head against your hand if it's ready for a gentle stroke.

43

CAT HISTORY

Cats were probably first domesticated in ancient Egypt. African wildcats came to hunt the easy prey around the grain supplies—and it didn't take the Egyptians long to appreciate the cat's usefulness. The wildcat gradually became a tame cat, picking up a dash of jungle cat along the way.

From pest-controller to pet was a small step, but the cat went further: it became a god! The Egyptians held many animals sacred. From about 1500 B.C., for more than a thousand years, Egypt worshiped a kindly cat goddess called Bastet, and her fierce sister, the lion-headed war goddess Sekhmet.

Egyptian cat mummy

Egyptian revival
Modern cat breeders produced the Egyptian Mau as a copy of cats in Egyptian wall paintings: graceful, leggy, and spotted, with big ears. The American version was bred from modern Egyptian cats and the British from Siamese crosses, so they look slightly different.

▲ Dead cats and kittens received the same treatment as dead pharaohs: they were made into mummies. These were then given as offerings to the cat goddess.

Bastet was shown as a seated cat (1) or as a cat-headed woman (2). Both Bastet and Sekhmet (3) could be lion-headed. Even the mighty sun god Ra took on cat form (4) to slay the Serpent of Darkness.

One legend tells how a cat earned the gratitude of Mary when it kept the Baby Jesus warm in the manger at Bethlehem. To this day, tabbies wear an "M" for Mary on their foreheads. Another legend links this mark with the Prophet Muhammad.

Myth and magic

In ancient Egypt cats were sacred animals and for centuries they remained linked to the supernatural. In the East, they were associated with both the Buddha and Muhammad. In the West, medieval Christians connected them with the Devil. Superstitions link cats with both good luck and bad, and they appear in folktales as powerful, sometimes kindly magicians.

The witch's cat

No self-respecting witch would be without a cat! Around 1600, a pet cat could prove you to be a witch. With its glow-in-the-dark eyes, the cat was clearly magical. Some people thought it was the Devil in animal form.

Lucky charms
In the United States and many European countries, black cats are considered unlucky. But in Britain they are said to bring good luck.

There are many myths and stories to explain how the cat was created. An Arabian legend describes how the cat's origins can be traced to the Flood. On board the Ark, Noah's pair of mice bred, and the vessel was soon overrun. When Noah asked the lion for help, the king of beasts sneezed. Two miniature lions sprang out of his nostrils and got to work mousing—they were the very first cats!

To the Vikings, cats were the beasts of the love goddess Freya. In Norse legend, her chariot is drawn by two great cats, sometimes said to be wildcats or lynxes.

Eastern cats inspired what is probably the world's oldest surviving cat book, a scroll from medieval Siam (now Thailand). The *Cat Book Poems* describes, in words and pictures, the 17 kinds of cat then known. They include the ancestors of Siamese and Burmese, as well as the silver-blue Korat (below), said to have fur with "tips like clouds and roots like silver."

Cats of the East

From Egypt, cats spread across the world. They were a great success in the East, making themselves at home in palaces and monasteries. It was here, centuries ago, that the first distinct breeds, including the Siamese and Burmese, evolved.

Like their Egyptian ancestors, Eastern cats remained slender, leggy, and long-headed. We still call cat breeds of this type Oriental, classing them apart from stockier Western cats. They also differ in character, most being more active, more people-oriented, and louder than other breeds!

Early Siamese had a squint, and a bent tail—acquired long ago in the line of duty. While bathing, Thai princesses hung their rings on the cat's tail. He went cross-eyed from watching the rings and bent his tail by tying it in a knot for safety. In most of today's Siamese—except for feral ones in Thailand—squints and kinked tails have disappeared.

This "Beckoning Cat" is a good luck charm in Japan. It depicts another ancient Eastern breed, the Japanese Bobtail, for centuries kept only by noblemen. This handsome stump-tailed cat is now popular in many countries.

Cats of the West

The cat spread across Europe during the Roman Empire.

Egyptians might have called it a god, but practical Romans knew a good mouser when they saw one! Neither royal nor sacred, the Western cats had to work for their living. As pest-control agents, however, they found a secure place in human homes—and then in human hearts. Today, most of our cats are loved pets rather than working breeds.

A new ingredient

Cats replaced tame mongooses as pest-controllers in Roman villas. They came in a choice of two colors. Along with the original tabby, blacks came on the scene in the first millennium B.C.

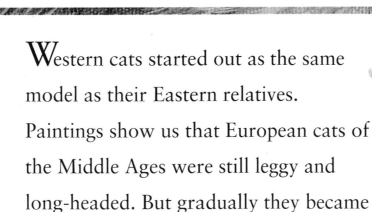

American Shorthair
Leggier than the British, descended from the cats of 17th-century settlers.

Western cats started out as the same model as their Eastern relatives. Paintings show us that European cats of the Middle Ages were still leggy and long-headed. But gradually they became stockier, with shorter legs and rounder heads. Modern European and American Shorthairs have a heavier build than their Oriental cousins— and pedigreed British Shorthairs are the stockiest of all. Perhaps due to their working ancestry, Western cats also have a more independent, if less determined, character—which doesn't stop them from making wonderful pets.

▲ **A trio of 13th-century ratters.**

British Shorthair
The pedigreed version— much stockier than non-pedigreed pets.

Exotic Shorthair
Bred in the 1950s, this cat has some of the Persian's shape, but short hair.

Tell no tails!
Originating on the Isle of Man in the Irish Sea, "rumpy" Manx cats are famous for not having tails. In fact, breeding (but not show) animals may have stubs ("rumpy-riser"), or short ("stumpy") or even full-length ("longy") tails.

ISLE OF MAN

40p Manx Cats

Scottish Fold
A cat with unusual ears which originated in Scotland in the 1960s.

▶ **The lean American Shorthair is probably closest to the ancestors of all the Western cats. Stockier cats developed later. Recent creations include the Exotic Shorthair and the Scottish Fold.**

Shaggy cat stories

Modern Persians (1) have an enormous coat. It's too much for the cat to take care of itself, so you shouldn't even think of having one of these beautiful animals unless you have time for daily grooming.

The Maine Coon (2) and the Norwegian Forest Cat (3) are longhairs, but not of the Persian type. Their thick, shaggy coats are needed for cold winters. Both are working breeds and are perfectly capable of taking care of their own coats.

The longhair story

The shorthair is the basic model of domestic cat. Longhairs first appeared in the East, and were introduced to Europe by travelers in the 1500s. These were slender, silky-coated Angora cats from Turkey. Later the rounder, fluffier Persian arrived from Persia (modern Iran). It was bred with other longhairs, including the Angora, which disappeared from the cat scene until recent times.

Luxury pets

An Italian, Pietro della Valle, is said to have brought some of Europe's first Angoras from Turkey in the 1500s. Described as "ash-colored, dun, and speckled, very beautiful to behold," they were soon in demand as luxury pets. Two centuries later, Persians were in and Angoras were out! The breed was revived in the 1960s—in two slightly different versions, American (from Turkish imports) and British (from long-coat Orientals).

Heavily-coated Persians and silky Angoras have been joined by a wide range of other longhairs. Some, like the Birman and the Siberian Forest Cat, developed over centuries as distinct breeds in their own countries. Others are modern creations. Since the 1960s, breeders have produced a growing number of longhaired versions of popular shorthair breeds (see right). We now have a wide variety of coat lengths, but all these handsome cats need daily brushing to keep their coats clean and healthy.

The handsome Abyssinian now comes in a longhaired version, the Somali.

The Cymric is a longhaired Manx with a thick, woolly undercoat.

The Tiffanie is a long-haired cross between a Burmese and Chinchilla.

The Balinese is a longhaired Siamese. Some colors are called Javanese.

Cat shows

The first cat show, held in London in 1871, was a big event in cat history. It was organized by British cat-lover Harrison Weir to make more people appreciate their pets' beauty. It was a huge success, and the result was the "invention" of the pedigreed cat. A cat's appearance was no longer taken for granted, and suddenly there was a reason to develop distinct breeds. The first were created mainly by dividing existing types of cat by color.

The first show

Cat breeds didn't really exist in 1871, so most classes were simply for different colors—mainly shorthairs. Even a Scottish wildcat was entered, but no one could coax it into the show pen!

At first, new kinds of cat appeared by accident: a breeder spotted an unusual color or coat type and decided to develop it. Later, new breeds were deliberately designed. A new breed has to be approved by show authorities, who must agree that it is genuinely different, worth adding to the collection, and free of health problems. If accepted, the new breed is shown on a trial basis for a while, until it is well established.

shape of tail

How a show cat matches up to the ideal for its breed is marked out of 100 points—as tests are marked out of 100 percent.

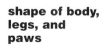

shape of body, legs, and paws

Shows today

These days, shows are highly organized. Usually, the cats are kept safe in numbered pens, so that the judge cannot guess who owns them. At some shows, the pens are highly decorated and very individual; at these there is a separate judging area.

B reeds continue to develop, but non-pedigreed cats still outnumber pedigreed. All in all, the best cat in the world is your own, and even an alley cat is descended from the Egyptian gods!

▶ Sorrel Abyssinian

New types may crop up in existing breeds. At first, Abyssinians only came in golden brown (Ruddy). Acceptance of the Sorrel opened the door for many more color varieties.

◀ Peke-faced Persian

Its flat Peke-like face is popular, but some cat-lovers find its runny eyes and snuffly breathing unacceptable.

A cat could earn ten points each for its coat and tail. How the points are divided varies from breed to breed and country to country.

shape of head and ears

size, shape, and color of eyes

color and condition of coat

◀ American Curl

Some breeds appear by chance. The American Curl is descended from a curly-eared stray found in California in 1981. This breed is not recognized outside the United States.

▼ Bengal

Breeders crossed domestic tabbies with wild leopard cats to create this beautiful new hybrid.

Cats in art

The cat's sleek shape has appealed to many artists, from Leonardo da Vinci to Andy Warhol, and each approaches the subject in their own style. Look out for Théophile Steinlen's elegant Parisian cat posters, Louis Wain's comical costumed cats and Foujita Tsugouharu's strokable Japanese drawings.

Book illustrators have produced a rich collection of cat images, too. Arthur Rackham is famous for the black-and-white drawings he created for *Dick Whittington* and *The Owl and the Pussycat*. Cat stories feature everything from cuddly picture-book kittens to wildcats and wonderful fairy-tale creations.

◄ **One of the best-known fictional felines is the Cheshire Cat from Lewis Carroll's *Alice in Wonderland*. His grin isn't very catlike, but his disappearing trick certainly is!**

◄ **British artist Louis Wain is famous for showing very human cats!**

▼ **Artist Tony Wood had fun with the curving lines of his cat teapot.**

▼ **This etching by George Cruikshank illustrates an old saying, "raining cats, dogs...and pitchforks."**

► **In folktales, cats often appear as wise helpers. Puss-in-Boots wins the hand of a beautiful princess for the poor master who inherits him.**

▼ **Quentin Blake's *Dick Whittington* shows the cat that helped Dick to rise from rags to riches, and become Lord Mayor of London.**

Famous cats

Cats play a starring role in our lives, and in our imaginations. Writers, artists, and film-makers have all been inspired by them. Joy and George Adamson's lion friends were immortalized in books and on the silver screen, but most famous cats are made up. As in life, cats in fiction can be snooty, cuddly, and even funny! They range from Garfield, the lazy cartoon eating-machine, to the madcap story-book host of Dr. Seuss's *Cat in the Hat*. And T.S. Eliot created a whole range of cat characters for the poems in his *Old Possum's Book of Practical Cats*.

▼ **In 1919, Felix became the first feline movie star. He featured in hundreds of cartoons, including the first animation "talkie," and was the first moving image shown on TV.**

▶ **Morris was the most successful advertising cat of all time and won a Patsy Award for his acting.**

▲ *Tom and Jerry* **cartoons have been family favorites since 1939.**

Movie stars

Cat-lovers can have a field day at the movies. Some stars are mainly decorative. Solomon, a beautiful Chinchilla cat, sat in the lap of several James Bond villains. But others are talented actors and have more active roles. Syn the Siamese (*That Darn Cat*, 1965) and Orangey the ginger longhair (*Rhubarb*, 1951) were two stars whose performances won them Patsy Awards for Best Animal Actor.

◀ **Cats are so appealing that they are used to sell us all sorts of products.**

Cats sell!

Morris, a handsome tom, was such a hit in cat-food ads that he became a Hollywood star. He even ran for President. Cats make great commercials, and not just for cat food. Advertisers use them to sell products ranging from carpets to chocolates.

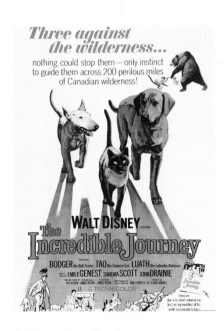

▲ **When Syn the Siamese appeared in** *The Incredible Journey,* **he had to costar with two dogs!**

Breeds

Pedigreed cats are considered by some to be the aristocrats of the cat world. It is little more than a century since Harrison Weir "invented" the pedigreed cat, yet today there are nearly one hundred breeds. Thirty of these are longhaired breeds and the rest are shorthaired. Shorthairs can be split into two groups, depending on their body shape: stocky (Western) or slender (Eastern).

Some pedigreed cats come in just one color—the Havana Brown is only ever brown and the Bombay is always black. But the Persian, for example, can be one of over one hundred different shades and patterns!

Just to add to the confusion, two breeds share the same name! One Turkish Van (the "classic") still lives by Lake Van in its native Turkey; the other has been bred in the West.

LONGHAIRS
1 Persian
2 Himalayan
3 Maine Coon
4 Norwegian Forest Cat
5 Ragdoll
6 Balinese
7 Somali
8 Birman
9 Cymric
10 Angora
11 American Curl
12 Turkish Van
13 Turkish Van (classic)
14 Tiffanie

Glossary

agouti A speckled "salt-and-pepper" ground color; seen in Abyssinians and between the dark bands of a tabby.

albino White with red eyes; a rare color in cats.

AOC Any Other Color (a show class).

AOV Any Other Variety (a show class).

Asian Cat of Burmese type but with a different coat color or length, seen in Burmillas, Burmoirés, and Tiffanies.

awn hairs Very short, bristly hairs; the middle layer of a cat's coat.

bicolor White cat with bold patches of color. Show cats must have an even pattern of patches.

blaze White stripe running down the forehead and nose, as in Tortoiseshell-and-Whites.

bloodline A cat's ancestry.

blue Gray coloring from slate-gray to pale, bluish gray.

breed Class of cats with similar appearance and related ancestry, for example, Persian.

brindling A random mixture of hairs of different colors in a cat's coat (usually a show fault).

brush Tail of a long-haired cat.

calico A white cat with colored patches.

cameo Having white hairs with red, cream, or tortoiseshell tips.

canines The long, sharp teeth near the front of the mouth, used for catching and killing prey.

carnassials Ridged, sharp-edged teeth at the back of the mouth, used for gripping and tearing food.

castration Neutering a male by the surgical removal of the testes.

catnip Garden plant that is irresistible to many cats.

cattery (1) Place where cats are cared for in their owners' absence. (2) Place where cats are bred.

cobby Stocky, short-bodied, short-legged, and compact.

condition The state of a cat's health, fitness, and grooming.

conformation Body shape and size, characteristic of a breed.

crossbred A non-pedigreed cat.

crossbreeding Mating two different breeds or varieties.

dam Mother cat.

dewclaw Claw on the inside of the foreleg, somewhat like a thumb.

dilute Paler version of a basic color, such as blue or cream.

double coat Coat in which the underlying awn hairs are the same length as the top layer of guard hairs.

down hairs Short, fine hairs; the bottom layer of the cat's coat.

entire Not neutered.

feral Domestic cat that has gone wild.

flehmen Lipcurling expression made when air is drawn into the Jacobsen's organ.

frill The ruff of fur around a longhair's face.

fur ball Hair swallowed by cats while grooming, that is usually coughed up.

gauntlets White "socks" extending partly up the legs, seen on the hind legs of Birmans.

ghost markings Faint, tabby markings sometimes seen in solid-colored cats, especially in kittens.

gloves White paws below dark legs, seen on the forepaws of Birmans.

guard hairs Long, straight hairs; the top layer of a cat's coat.

inbreeding Breeding closely related cats (such as a brother and sister).

incisors Small front teeth, used for tearing food and for grooming.

Jacobsen's organ Special sense organ in the roof of the mouth that "tastes" scents in the air.

jowls Heavy cheek folds, seen especially in toms.

kink Bend in the tail (a show fault).

kitten Cat under nine months old.

lavender Pale, pinkish-gray color.

linebreeding Breeding cats that are related within the last three generations.

litter Kittens born at the same time to the same mother.

litter box Toilet tray used indoors.

locket White patch under the chin.

mask A face darker than the rest of the cat, seen in Siamese.

brush

feral

catnip

gloves

blaze

brindling

double coat

mitts White paws, extending farther than gloves, but not as far as gauntlets—for example, in Mitted Ragdolls.

neuter (1) To make an animal incapable of breeding by the surgical removal of its reproductive organs. (2) A castrated male or spayed female.

crossbred

nictitating membrane Film at the inner corner of each eye, which extends across the eye when the cat is sick.

nose leather The bare skin around a cat's nostrils.

odd-eyed Having eyes of different colors.

oriental Breeds with long bodies, fine bones, and wedge-shaped heads.

outcross To breed unrelated cats together.

pads Leathery skin on the soles of the paws.

pedigreed cat Purebred cat whose birth has been registered with an official cat club.

odd-eyed

pen Display cage in which a show cat stays when it is not being judged.

penciling Delicate markings like pencil lines on the face of a tabby.

pointed Having points of a darker color than the rest of the body.

points A cat's ears, muzzle, tail, and feet.

prefix Registered name of a breeding cattery, attached to the name of each kitten born there.

points

purebred A cat whose parents belong to the same breed.

queen Female cat.

quick Vein and nerves in a cat's claw.

rangy Long-bodied and long-legged.

recognition Official acceptance of a breed for show purposes.

registration Recording of a kitten's birth and parentage with an official cat club.

rex Having a short, curly coat without guard hairs.

rumpy A Manx without a tail.

rumpy-riser A Manx with a tiny, stubbed tail.

shaded Having a coat of pale hairs that gradually darken toward the tips.

shell Having a coat of pale hairs that are colored at the very tips.

show Exhibition of cats. The animals are judged according to a standard of points, and the winners are awarded prizes.

sire Father cat.

smoke Having a coat of dark hairs that are pale at the base.

solid Having a coat of one color.

spaying Neutering a female by the surgical removal of the ovaries and uterus.

spraying Marking territory with urine, usually by entire males.

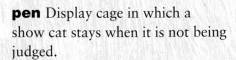
sire

squint Eye deformity, giving a cross-eyed look; sometimes found in Siamese.

standard of points Blueprint by which show cats are judged.

stop A marked dent in the bridge of the nose, just below the eyes.

stud (1) Tom kept for breeding. (2) Breeding cattery.

stumpy A Manx with a short tail.

stumpy

ticked Hair banded in two or three colors, as in Abyssinians.

tipped Having the ends of each hair a different color from the rest, as in Chinchillas.

tom Male cat.

tipped

tortoiseshell A three-colored cat, usually black, red, and cream.

type Physical appearance of a cat (or breed) in relation to the breed standard.

undercoat Short, woolly fur made up of awn hairs and down hairs.

usual Original color of a breed, before varieties were developed.

variant Cat bred from two pedigreed cats that differs from the breed standard and so cannot enter a championship at shows.

variety Color form within a breed.

vibrissae Whiskers on a cat's head and wrists, adapted to sense what they touch.

whip tail Long, thin tail tapering to a point at the end; seen in Oriental Whites.

whip tail

Index

Acknowledgments

The publishers would like to thank the following
illustrators for their contributions to this book:

Andrew Beckett (Illustration) 32–33; **John Butler** 10–11, 24–25; **Jim Channel**
(Bernard Thornton Artists) 5*br*, 6*tr*, 7, 11*tr*, 12*bl*, 15*mr*, 17*mr*, 18*tr*, 19*tr*,
21*bl*, 27*tl*, 29*ml*; **Paul Cox** 25*t*, 42–43; **Sandra Doyle** 9*br*, 12*tl*, 13*tr*;
Madeleine Floyd 26–27, 31*t*; **Rachel Fuller** 16–17; **Lynda Gray** 18–19, 44–45;
Martin Hargreaves (Illustration) 4–5; **Sue Hellard** (The Organisation) 36*mr*,
37*ml*, 39, 41*m*, 43*r*; **Kate Hodges** 60–61; **Christian Hook** 58–59; **Malcolm
McGregor** 13*br*, 15*t*, 37*t*, 44*bl*, 51*r*, 52*l*, 55*r*; **Tony McSweeney** 46*tl*; **James
Marsh** 49; **Danuta Mayer** 50–51, 52–53; **Karen Murray** 28–29; **Liz Pyle**
46–47; **Mike Rowe** (Wildlife Art Agency) 12–13, 36, 54–55;
Claudia Saraceni 20–21; **Paul Stagg** (Virgil Pomfret Agency) 14–15, 40–41;
Eric Tenney 8–9, 30–31; **Helen Ward** (Virgil Pomfret Agency) 22–23, 34–35;
Ann Winterbotham 6*b*, 14*bl*, 16*ml*, 34*l*, 38, 39*tr*, 40*br*, 41*bl*.

Marmalade the Multifaceted Cat by **Kate Hodges**
Decorative border by **Paul Stagg** (Virgil Pomfret Agency)

The publishers would also like to thank the following for supplying
photographs for this book:

Liz Artindale: 30*tr*; **Bridgeman Art Library:** 25*mr* *A Musical Gathering of
Cats* Ferdinand Van Kessell; 31*br* *The Cat* Tsugouharu Foujita; 32*b* *Playing
With Mother* Horatio Cauldery; 44*m*; 56*ml* *Cat's Tea Party* Louis Wain
(courtesy V&A Museum); 56*m* (courtesy Bonhams); 56*bl* *Raining Cats, Dogs
and Pitchforks!* George Cruikshank; 56*br* *Dick Whittington and his cat*
Quentin Blake, an illustration from *Rhyme Stew* by Roald Dahl (courtesy
Chris Beetle's, London); **British Library:** 51*tl* *Ms. Harleian Bestiary*; **British
Museum:** 8*bl* "Paresse" from *Des Chats* Théophile Steinlen; **Dragon News &
Picture Agency:** 20*mr*; **Mary Evans Picture Library:** 8–9 *Animals in Motion*
Eadward Muybridge; 46*br*; 54*bl*; 56*tr* *The Nursery Alice* Sir John Tenniel;
56*mr* *Puss-in-Boots*; **Paul Franklin:** 7*t*; **Glenturret Distillery:** 27*tr*; **Ronald
Grant Archive:** 57*bl*, *m* & *br* (courtesy Walt Disney); **Marc Henrie, Asc:** 55*tl*;
Magnum Photos: 10*m* *Dali Atomicus* Philippe Halsman; **Marlborough
Gallery, NY:** 40*bl* *Cat* © Fernando Botero; **Nickleodeon Animation:** 41*mr*;
Oxford Scientific Films: 33*l*; **Photofest:** 57*tr*; **Retrograph Archive Collection:**
47*t*; 57*tm*; **Scala:** 17*tr*; **Paul Sehault/Eye Ubiquitous:** 48*r*; **Roger Tabor:** 48*tl*;
Telegraph Colour Library/Al Satterwhite: 26*tl*; **Topham Picture Library:** 42*m*.